Cissie Palmer

Community BUILDERS

Cissie Palmer

Community BUILDERS

Putting Wealth to Work

by Judy
Alter

(P)

Children's Press®
A Division of Grolier Publishing
New York London Hong Kong Sydney
Danbury, Connecticut

Photo Credits

Photographs ©: Archive Photos: 12 (Jacob A. Riis), 9, 15, 27; Art Resource: 24, 45 (Erich Lessing); Chicago Historical Society: 13 (J. Carbutt), cover, 2, 43 (Steffens), 6, 11, 17, 18, 25, 40; Corbis-Bettmann: 8, 22, 33, 38; MIT Museum: 36 top; Smiley's Studio, Fort Worth , Texas: 48; Stock Montage, Inc.: back cover, 16, 31; The Image Works: 44 (McLaughlin); UPI/Corbis-Bettmann: 3, 20, 28, 29, 34, 36 bottom, 42.

Reading Consultant
Linda Cornwell, Learning Resource Consultant
Indiana Department of Education

Visit Children's Press on the Internet at:
http://publishing.grolier.com

Library of Congress Cataloging-in-Publication Data

Alter, Judy, 1938–
    Cissie Palmer : putting wealth to work / by Judy Alter.
        p. cm. — (Community builders)
    Includes bibliographical references and index.
    Summary: A biography of the wealthy Chicago socialite who used her money to advance worthy city causes and to improve the lives of working women.
    ISBN: 0-516-20972-8 (lib.bdg.)   0-516-26345-5 (pbk.)
    1. Palmer, Bertha (Honoré) 1849–1918—Juvenile literature. 2. Social reformers—Illinois—Chicago—Biography—Juvenile literature. 3. Feminism—United States—History—Juvenile literature. [1. Palmer, Bertha (Honoré) 1849-1918. 2. Reformers. 3. Feminism. 4. Women—Biography.] I. Title. II. Series.
HV99.C4A48 1998
361.7'4'092—dc21
[B]   97-43216
                                                                                  CIP
                                                                                   AC

Contents

Cissie Palmer as she looked in 1893, during
the World's Columbian Exposition

Chapter ONE

Cissie Palmer

Have you ever been to a state or county fair where there was a display of products that were made by women? Did those products include jams, jellies, cakes, and pies? Was there a separate area that included displays of machinery or industry and was visited mostly by men?

At the 1893 World's Columbian Exposition in Chicago, Illinois, Cissie Palmer proved that women produce much more than pies, cakes, jams, and jellies. The exposition (a large fair) was held to celebrate the four-hundredth anniversary of Christopher Columbus's arrival in North America.

Women's Work

At the time of the 1893 World's Columbian Exposition, most Americans believed that women should stay at home and raise their children. (Women were not even allowed to vote in local or national elections.) The only "proper" work for women was teaching or sewing. The poorest women worked in factories, but they were both pitied and looked down on.

In this 1898 photograph, a schoolteacher leads her students in a drawing lesson.

Chicago, Illinois, in 1890—the city where Cissie Palmer spent most of her life

Cissie served as president of the exposition's Board of Lady Managers. She arranged for a women's building that was designed, constructed, decorated, and managed by women. Women, she insisted, were not just cooks, seamstresses, and mothers. They were also architects, construction workers, contractors, sculptors, and artists.

The Women's Building was Cissie Palmer's triumph, but she had spent many years working in Chicago for the recognition of women. Although she was married to a wealthy man and did not need to

9

earn money by working, Cissie fought to improve the lives of working women. Cissie Palmer left her mark on Chicago, though today she is little recognized either nationally or in her city. There is no statue honoring her efforts. The mansion her husband built for her on North Lake Shore Drive was torn down in 1950 to make room for high-rise apartments.

The Art Institute of Chicago contains the Palmer Collection, but the paintings were donated by Cissie's sons long after her death. The archives (a collection of historically important records, letters, and documents) at the institute contain articles about Cissie Palmer, and some of the letters she wrote and received. The most striking monument to her is the Palmer House hotel, built in the 1870s by her husband Potter. Today, it continues to operate as a fine hotel.

Cissie Palmer is one among many women who made great contributions to their local and national communities during their lifetime, but are sometimes accidently overlooked by history. This is the story of Cissie's life and work.

Chapter TWO

A Sheltered Childhood

Cissie Palmer was born Bertha Honoré on May 22, 1849, in Louisville, Kentucky. When she was six years old, her father, Henry Honoré, moved his family to Chicago because it was a young, growing city with many business opportunities. Bertha had one sister, Ida, and four

Bertha Honoré (later nicknamed "Cissie") as a young girl, about 1860

The sewing class that Bertha and her sister attended was much like this one, which took place about 1880.

younger brothers. Bertha and Ida were educated at convents (girls' schools run by nuns from the Roman Catholic Church). There, they were taught subjects including French, flower arranging, and sewing.

In 1862, when Bertha was thirteen years old, Potter Palmer came to a party at her family's home. Years later, he said that he decided that night to wait for Bertha to grow up so that he could marry her. Palmer, who was twenty-three years older than Bertha, gave her the nickname "Cissie."

Bertha went east to finish her education in Washington, D.C. When she returned in 1867, she was formally introduced to Chicago society at a party called a debut. After that, Potter Palmer began to court her. They were married on July 29, 1870.

12

Potter Palmer

Potter Palmer arrived in Chicago in 1852 from the eastern United States. He opened a general store and was known for being a good businessman. He was also known for paying special attention to his customers. He knew most of his female customers by name, as well as the kinds of fabrics, gloves, and clothing they preferred. During the Civil War (1861–65), Potter invested in wool and cotton and made his fortune. After the war, he invested in real estate. By the time Potter married Cissie, he was one of Chicago's wealthiest men.

Chapter THREE

Wife of an Important Businessman

Potter Palmer's wedding gift to Cissie was to be the Palmer House hotel, which was being built at the time of their marriage. But in 1871, when Cissie and Potter had been married only a year, the Palmer House was destroyed in Chicago's Great Fire. At the time, Potter Palmer was away. Cissie was alone in their country home on the edge of the city, but she was not hurt.

**The Palmer House hotel in 1870, before it was
destroyed in the Great Fire**

The Great Chicago Fire

Chicago's Great Fire began on October 8, 1871, and burned for three days. Three hundred people died, 90,000 were left homeless, and 17,000 buildings were destroyed. At the time, it was the worst fire in U.S. history. For years, it was believed that a cow belonging to Mrs. Catharine O'Leary kicked over a lantern in its barn and started the fire. But no one knows how the fire actually began.

The cause of the Great Chicago Fire is still a mystery.

This photograph of the block that contained many of Potter's buildings was taken just a few days after the fire.

Potter Palmer owned thirty-two of the buildings that were lost in the fire, including the Palmer House. When he considered leaving the city to start over in a new city, Cissie told him she believed it was the duty of every Chicagoan to stay and help rebuild the city. The plans for the Palmer House had been saved because they were buried under the building for safekeeping. Potter used them to rebuild it.

The year 1874 was a big one for the Palmers. Their first son, Honoré, was born in February. Cissie's sister Ida married the son of U.S. president Ulysses S. Grant. And the Palmer family moved into Potter's hotel. The new Palmer House was Chicago's most elegant hotel. It was noted for its restaurant's delicious steaks, the elevator that delivered guests to all eight floors, and the barbershop that had silver dollars laid in its floor. Potter Palmer personally

The lobby of the Palmer House, which was considered the finest hotel in Chicago

Chicago, Illinois

Chicago is one of the largest cities in the United States. It is a well-known trade, industry, and transportation center for the Midwest. Located on the southwestern shore of Lake Michigan, it is home to the Sears Tower, one of the world's tallest buildings.

Cissie Palmer (left), with a few members of the Chicago Women's Club

greeted each guest. Cissie was frequently seen visiting in the lobby. In the evenings, when Potter came to their apartment on the eighth floor, Cissie listened carefully as he discussed the day's business. She learned a great deal about business from her husband. Meanwhile, their second son, Potter, was born in October 1875.

As the wife of one of Chicago's wealthiest men, Cissie Palmer could have simply gone to teas and luncheons and filled her life with pleasure. But she believed that having a lot of money made a person responsible to those with less money. Both she and her husband were known for generosity with their money and their time.

Within a year of the Great Fire, Potter Palmer

20

pledged $100,000 to help build a new YMCA in the city. Cissie joined the Women's Christian Temperance Union, which fought against the selling and drinking of alcoholic beverages. She worked at Hull House, the famous settlement house founded by Jane Addams to help newcomers from other countries learn the ways of the United States. She also joined the Chicago Women's Club, which studied social problems such as the hard conditions suffered by working women.

Although most American women at that time did not work outside the home, many women in Chicago worked as secretaries, accountants, cashiers, typists, sales clerks, and factory workers. Cissie began to invite women who worked in factories to meet at her house. With Cissie's help, the women who worked in hat-making factories organized to demand better working conditions, such as shorter hours, higher salaries, and more light and fresh air in the factories. Cissie Palmer attended her share of fancy society parties, but she was as much at home with working women as she was with rich women.

Potter's Castle was located at 1350 North Lake Shore Drive in Chicago. Today, the street remains one of the most prestigious places to live in the United States.

Chapter FOUR

Potter's Castle

In 1882, Potter Palmer began building a new home for his family. He chose an empty strip of property on Chicago's north lake shore. After he built his house, the area became the city's most fashionable neighborhood to live in. It is still fashionable today. It took three years to build what became known as Potter's Castle, a three-story building of granite and sandstone with an 80-foot (24-meter) tower and a three-story entrance hall. With marble floors, priceless tapestries, and Impressionist paintings, it was the most luxurious home in Chicago. The castle

Impressionism

Impressionism was one of Cissie Palmer's favorite styles of painting. Impressionism developed in France in the 1870s and 1880s. Artists such as Monet, Renoir, and Degas believed that ideas were more powerful than reality. Their paintings feature dabs of brightly colored paint. When seen from a distance, the dabs blend into trees, flowers, landscapes, or people. Cissie Palmer is largely responsible for introducing Impressionism to Chicago.

This Impressionist painting by French artist Claude Monet was completed in 1872.

stood until 1950, when it was torn down in order to construct apartment buildings.

By 1890, Cissie Palmer was, at forty years old, the queen of Chicago society and married to a millionaire. She had two sons, lived in a huge mansion, and owned a collection of fine art. She had an enormous wardrobe and many expensive jewels. But Cissie needed to be active in her community. Her greatest achievement was just ahead—the World's Columbian Exposition.

The main gallery of Potter's Castle displayed much of the fine art the Palmers owned.

Chapter FIVE

The Board of Lady Managers

Cissie didn't know it, but in the late 1880s, planning was taking place that would change her life. The United States government decided to celebrate the four-hundredth anniversary of Columbus's arrival in North America with a world's exposition. There, the wonderful things that were produced in the United States would be displayed. The exposition would also include displays from other countries. Officials from New York, St. Louis, Missouri,

26

Chicagoans knew that the World's Columbian Exposition would draw millions of visitors to their city.

and Washington, D.C., each wanted the exposition to be held in their city. When Chicago was chosen, many people were angry. They claimed that Chicago was a boring, ugly city full of saloons, and had no law and order. But Chicagoans felt differently. They believed that the exposition would be a chance for their city to gain national attention.

The World's Columbian Exposition

The World's Columbian Exposition of 1893 was best known for its White City, a collection of buildings that looked like ancient Greek temples. The White City surrounded a series of lagoons, waterways, bridges, fountains, and walkways. It included buildings for agriculture, machinery, electricity, and mining. Nearby stood the Women's Building, as well as buildings that were devoted to fine arts, photography, transportation, and children. The most famous scientists, artists, architects, historians, and lawyers

The buildings of the White City were decorated with columns, pillars, stone carvings, and statues.

The newly invented Ferris wheel held thirty-six cars which, when fully loaded, could carry more than two thousand people.

of the day came to the exposition to discuss their contributions to science and industry. The exposition was also known for the Midway, a strip of displays and shops that included balloon rides, belly dancers, and the native foods and entertainment of various countries. The world's first Ferris wheel was located on the Midway.

Almost twenty-eight million people visited the exposition during the five months it was open. By the time it closed, Chicago had become one of the most important cities in the United States.

The committee of men who planned the exposition thought women's work was less important and should be displayed separately from the important work of men. They decided on a separate women's building and appointed a Board of Lady Managers with two women representing each state in the United States. At the first meeting, Cissie Palmer was elected president of the board.

Cissie faced many difficulties in her role. One was keeping all the women happy, which was impossible. Cissie had to deal with several different groups of women, all with different ideas for the women's building. One group was the suffragettes, women who campaigned for women's right to vote. They called themselves the "Isabellas" in honor of Spain's Queen Isabella, who sent Columbus to North America. The Isabellas thought Cissie would accept the traditional role of women as housewives and mothers rather than fight for equal rights for women. Cissie Palmer, however, was a supporter of women's rights. She believed women should be paid

Cissie Palmer in 1893, while serving as president
of the Board of Lady Managers

as much as men for doing the same work. She also believed that women should have the right to vote. But Cissie didn't like the ways of some suffragettes. She didn't like the way they bobbed their hair (cut in a short style) and wore bloomers (loose trousers gathered at the knee or the ankle). At the time, both practices were considered shocking. Cissie also did not like the loud, public protests the suffragettes often organized.

Suffrage

The word "suffrage" means "the right to vote." At the time of the Columbian Exposition, women in the United States were not allowed to vote. Most men at that time—and many women—believed that women had no place in government. For years, women insisted that they be allowed to vote. They were finally granted suffrage in 1920, when the 19th Amendment to the Constitution was adopted.

This 1892 illustration shows the bloomers and short hair that became popular with the suffragettes.

The Isabellas wanted women's products mixed in with exhibits of men's work at the exposition. Cissie thought that would result in women's work being overlooked. Then, the Isabellas wanted their own separate exhibit. Cissie explained that this was impossible because there was no building for them.

Next, two organizations of African-American women—the Women's Columbian Association and the Women's Columbian Auxiliary Association—wanted separate exhibits. Cissie explained that if this was allowed, each nationality would want to have its own exhibit. Cissie encountered so many problems that Potter Palmer told her that it was not the men who would destroy the women's exhibit, but the women themselves with their constant bickering. With patience and persistence, however, Cissie

**The Women's Building at the 1893
World's Columbian Exposition**

was finally able to present an idea for a women's building on which all the women agreed—but she continued to struggle to make all the women work together peacefully.

The Women's Building itself became Cissie's next problem. A world-famous male architect was chosen to design the building. Cissie protested that a woman should design it. She was told that there were no important women architects. So, in 1891, Cissie organized a competition for women to submit their designs for the building. A grand prize $1,000 would be awarded to the winner. A young woman named Sophia Hayden, who had studied architecture at the Massachusetts Institute of Technology, won the competition. But still another problem arose when Sophia came to Chicago. She was inexperienced and difficult to work with. Cissie Palmer was embarrassed, but work continued on the building Sophia designed. Another young female sculptor named Enid Yandell was chosen to design a portion of the roof garden.

Sophia Hayden, born about 1868 in Santiago, Chile, was the first woman to complete the Massachusetts Institute of Technology's four-year architecture course.

England's Queen Victoria reigned for sixty-three years (1837–1901), longer than any other British monarch.

Cissie travelled to Europe to get the support of women from other countries. Her job was difficult because governments in England, France, and other European countries believed that a woman's place was in the home. But Cissie eventually won the support of England's Queen Victoria and the French Minister of Commerce. Many other countries also promised to send exhibits for the exposition.

Grover Cleveland, who served as the nation's twenty-second and twenty-fourth president, was the featured speaker at the exposition's opening on May 1, 1893.

Chapter SIX

The Exposition Opens

On April 29, 1893, the Board of Lady Managers gathered publicly to give thanks for the gifts to their building. These gifts included art and furniture, including a turquoise-studded table from New Mexico and a chair made from buffalo horns that was given by the state of Kansas.

On May 1, 1893, President Grover Cleveland opened the exposition by pushing a button that set off the lights and fountains of the White City. Then the women had their own opening ceremony in their building. The poetry and music at the women's ceremony were all composed by women.

Thousands of women visited the Women's Building during the five-month exposition. They viewed the objects on display and ate in the roof garden restaurant. Cissie saw to it that all the women who wanted to could attend. She gave some of her gowns to Chicago's settlement houses, so poor women would

Visitors to the Women's Building enjoy the view of the fairgrounds from the balcony.

The End of the Exposition

The exposition ended on an unpleasant note: Chicago's mayor, Carter Harrison, was shot and killed by a city employee the night before the October 31 closing ceremonies.

The buildings of the exposition also met a sad fate. Made of plaster, they were never meant to be permanent. They quickly fell apart in Chicago's harsh winter weather. During the winter of 1894, many homeless people lived in the decaying buildings until one night, the buildings burned down.

Today, the only exposition building that survives is the former Palace of Fine Arts, which now houses Chicago's Museum of Science and Industry. It is constructed of marble.

Potter Palmer died in 1902, at the age of seventy-six.

have something nice to wear. She sent carriages for elderly or sick women and paid for folding wicker wheelchairs for them to tour the exposition. She gave luncheons for the girls who worked as guides in the building. She even served as godmother to an Eskimo baby born during the exposition.

Through her work with the World's Columbian Exposition, Cissie Palmer advanced the cause of women and helped bring national attention to her beloved city of Chicago. Shortly after the exposition

Cissie Palmer shortly after her husband's death

closed, Cissie Palmer sailed to Europe. For the rest of her life, she and Potter spent much of their time away from the United States.

After Potter died in 1902, Cissie lived the last years of her life in Florida. She died in 1918, at the age of sixty-eight. Cissie's reputation rests on her achievements in Chicago—working for fair treatment of women and, most important, being responsible for the Women's Building and the Board of Lady Managers at the World's Columbian Exposition.

In Your Community

Is a state or county fair held each year near your home? Does it include a women's exhibit? What kinds of things are displayed? How do the men's and women's exhibits differ? If you could talk to Cissie Palmer, what would you tell her about the things you saw?

Cissie did much to bring Impressionist art to Chicago. Do you live near an art museum? Ask an adult to take you for a visit. Look

Timeline

1826	1849	1852	1855	1861–1865	1862	1870	1871	1874

1826 — Potter Palmer is born.

1849 — Bertha Honoré is born in Louisville, Kentucky.

1852 — Potter Palmer arrives in Chicago.

1855 — Henry Honoré moves his family to Chicago, Illinois.

1861–1865 — Civil War; Potter Palmer makes his fortune.

1862 — Cissie and Potter meet at an Honoré family party.

1870 — Cissie and Potter are married on July 29.

1871 — Great Chicago Fire destroys Palmer House; it is later rebuilt.

1874 — Cissie and Potter's son, Honoré, is born in February.

for paintings that feature Impressionism. Look closely at an Impressionist painting. What does it look like? Back away slowly from the painting. Now what do you see? (If you don't live near an art museum, visit your local library. The librarian will be able to help you find books with examples of Impressionist art.)

Cissie Palmer gave her gowns to needy women so they would look nice at the exposition. Do you have any clothes that you don't wear anymore? Look for a community organization that takes donations of unused clothes. Ask your family and friends to donate some, too.

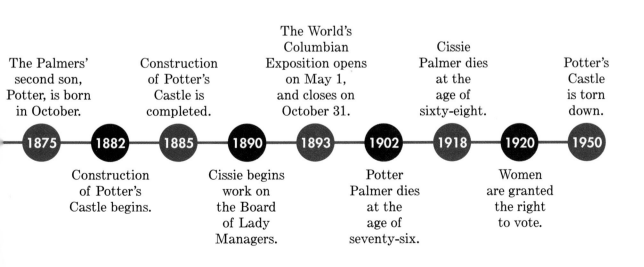

1875 — The Palmers' second son, Potter, is born in October.

1882 — Construction of Potter's Castle begins.

1885 — Construction of Potter's Castle is completed.

1890 — Cissie begins work on the Board of Lady Managers.

1893 — The World's Columbian Exposition opens on May 1, and closes on October 31.

1902 — Potter Palmer dies at the age of seventy-six.

1918 — Cissie Palmer dies at the age of sixty-eight.

1920 — Women are granted the right to vote.

1950 — Potter's Castle is torn down.

To Find Out More

Here are some additional resources to help you learn more about Cissie Palmer, the city of Chicago, and the World's Columbian Exposition:

Books

Alter, Judy. *Meet Me at the Fair.* Franklin Watts, 1997.

Simon, Charnan. *Jane Addams: Pioneer Social Worker.* Children's Press, 1997.

Stein, R. Conrad. *Chicago.* Children's Press, 1997.

Organizations and Online Sites

Interactive Guide to the World's Columbian Exposition
http://users.vnet.net/schulman/Columbian/columbian.html
This site contains almost everything about the exposition, including historical photographs, exhibit prices, Famous Firsts, and more.

Web-Book of the World's Columbian Exposition
http://fly.hiwaay.net/~shancock/fair/1893.html
Includes detailed descriptions of life in the United States, especially Chicago, at the end of the 1800s, newspaper articles written by people who attended the fair, and historical photographs.

Palmer House Hilton
http://www.cityinsights.com/chpalm.htm
Here you'll find information about the old Palmer House, and links to the sites of famous museums and other great places to visit in Chicago.

Potter Palmer and Bertha Honoré Palmer
http://www.graveyards.com/graceland/palmer.html
Take a tour of Chicago's Graceland Cemetery, the Palmers' burial place. You'll find pictures of Cissie's and Potter's tombstone, and a brief history of their accomplishments.

Index

About the Author

Judy Alter was born in Chicago and has lived in Texas for thirty years. She is the mother of four grown children and is currently responsible for two large dogs and two cats. Now living in Fort Worth, she is the director of Texas Christian University Press. A novelist and children's author, Ms. Alter is a two-time winner of the Western Heritage (Wrangler) Award from the National Cowboy Hall of Fame.

Ms. Alter is the author of several books for Children's Press, including *Sam Houston: A Leader for Texas* (Community Builders) and *The Santa Fe Trail* (Cornerstones of Freedom).